Selections from

Harry Potter AND THE Deathly Hallows PART 2

5 FINGER

Music by BY ALEXANDRE DESPLAT
Arranged by Tom Gerou

CONTENTS

Alfred

Produced by
Alfred Music Publishing Co., Inc.
P.O. Box 10003
Van Nuys, CA 91410-0003
alfred.com

ISBN-10: 0-7390-8448-8
ISBN-13: 978-0-7390-8448-9

Lily's Theme
Main Theme from *Harry Potter and the Deathly Hallows, Part 2*

By Alexandre Desplat

Arr. by Tom Gerou

Optional Duet Accompaniment (Play solo part 1 octave higher than written.)

(duet continued)

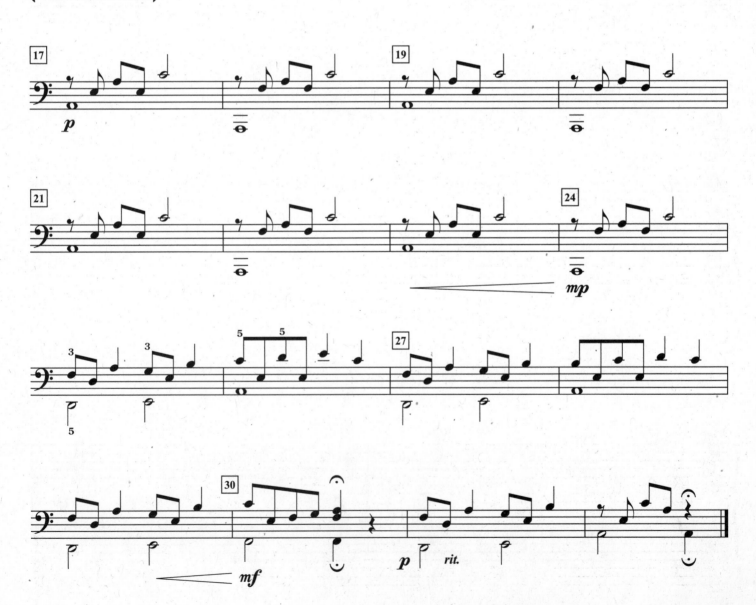

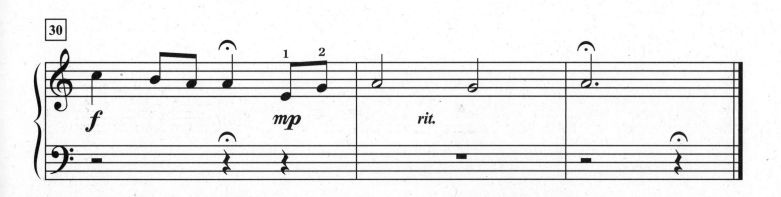

Statues
from *Harry Potter and the Deathly Hallows, Part 2*

By Alexandre Desplat

Arr. by Tom Gerou

Optional Duet Accompaniment (Play solo part 1 octave higher than written.)

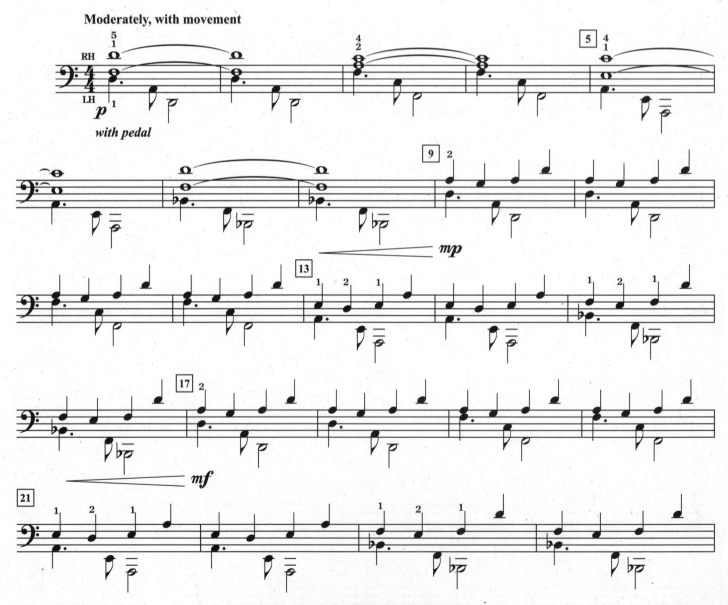

(duet continued)

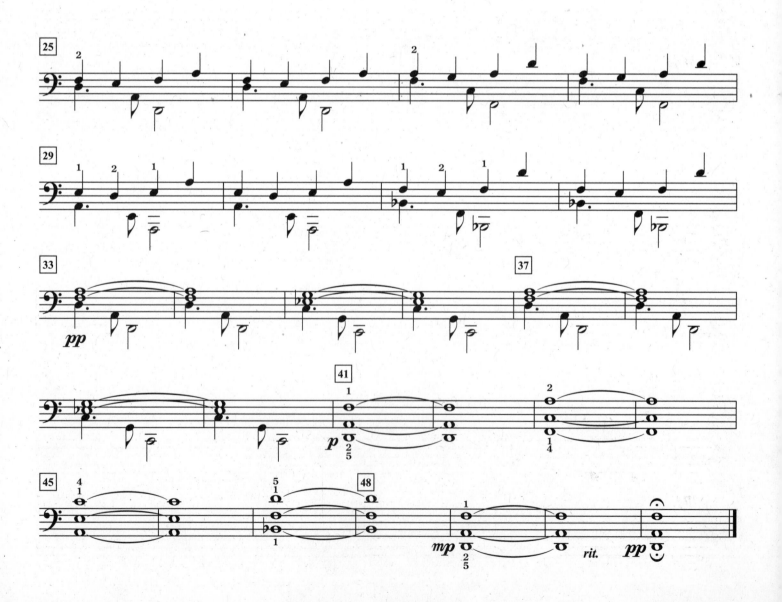

A New Beginning
from *Harry Potter and the Deathly Hallows, Part 2*

By Alexandre Desplat

Arr. by Tom Gerou

Optional Duet Accompaniment (Play solo part 1 octave higher than written.)

Neville the Hero

from *Harry Potter and the Deathly Hallows, Part 2*

By Alexandre Desplat
Arr. by Tom Gerou

Optional Duet Accompaniment (Play solo part 1 octave higher than written.)

Severus and Lily
from *Harry Potter and the Deathly Hallows, Part 2*

By Alexandre Desplat

Arr. by Tom Gerou

Optional Duet Accompaniment (Play solo part 1 octave higher than written.)

Harry's Sacrifice
from *Harry Potter and the Deathly Hallows, Part 2*

By Alexandre Desplat

Arr. by Tom Gerou

Optional Duet Accompaniment (Play solo part 1 octave higher than written.)

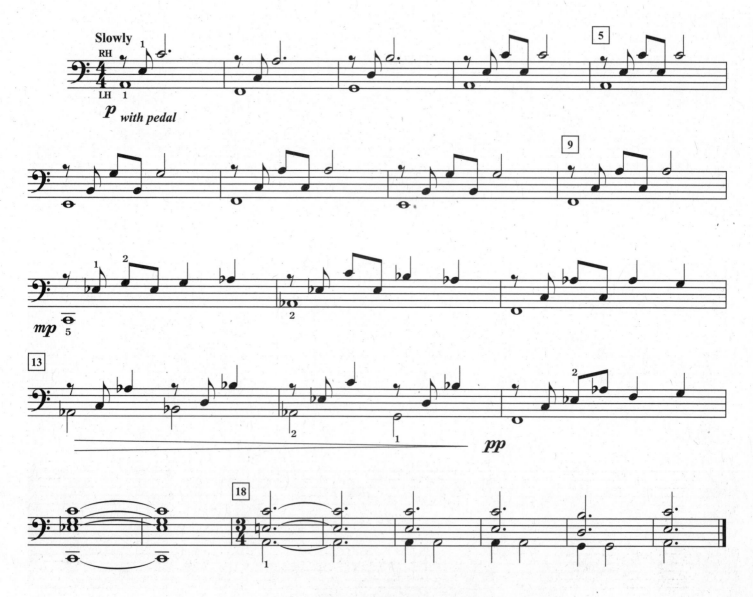

Lily's Lullaby
from *Harry Potter and the Deathly Hallows, Part 2*

By Alexandre Desplat
Arr. by Tom Gerou

Optional Duet Accompaniment (Play solo part 1 octave higher than written.)